TACTICAL SUMMARY of MACHINE GUN OPERATIONS

No. 1. October 1917

No. 2. November–December 1917

The Naval & Military Press Ltd

Published by the
The Naval & Military Press
in association with the Royal Armouries

Unit 10 Ridgewood Industrial Park,
Uckfield, East Sussex, TN22 5QE
Tel: +44 (0) 1825 749494
Fax: +44 (0) 1825 765701

MILITARY HISTORY AT YOUR FINGERTIPS
www.naval-military-press.com

ONLINE GENEALOGY RESEARCH
www.military-genealogy.com

ONLINE MILITARY CARTOGRAPHY
www.militarymaproom.com

The Library & Archives Department at the Royal Armouries Museum, Leeds, specialises in the history and development of armour and weapons from earliest times to the present day. Material relating to the development of artillery and modern fortifications is held at the Royal Armouries Museum, Fort Nelson.

For further information contact:
Royal Armouries Museum, Library, Armouries Drive,
Leeds, West Yorkshire LS10 1LT
Royal Armouries, Library, Fort Nelson, Down End Road, Fareham PO17 6AN

Or visit the Museum's website at
www.armouries.org.uk

In reprinting in facsimile from the original, any imperfections are inevitably reproduced and the quality may fall short of modern type and cartographic standards.

S.S.201   O.B./2007.

(Not to be taken into Action or Front Line Trenches).

TACTICAL SUMMARY of MACHINE GUN OPERATIONS

No. 1   **OCTOBER**

FOR OFFICIAL USE ONLY.

This Document is the property of H.B.M. Government, and the information in it is not to be communicated, either directly or indirectly, to the Press or any person not holding an official position in His Majesty's Service.

[ISSUED BY THE GENERAL STAFF.]

S.S. 201.]   [O.B. 2007.

Tactical Summary of Machine Gun Operations for October, 1917.

1. Nature of Information.

The material on which the present *résumé* is based consists of the brief list of tactical lessons noted in the Army Machine Gun Reports for October, Intelligence Summaries for the same month, and the narratives of particular operations from September 20th onwards.

Owing to the large measure of agreement which has been reached among Armies as to the principles of the tactical employment of Machine Guns in warfare against highly organized defences, no striking novelties are to be found in the tactical lessons mentioned in the Army reports. On the other hand, the narrative of particular operations shews manifold variation in detail, and sheds fresh light on the application of these agreed principles to the special kind of warfare that was experienced in the fight for the Passchendaele Ridge.

2. Intelligence Publications.

In the daily summaries and special publications issued by the General Staff, Intelligence, the following facts stand out :—

(a) There is evidence that the enemy is beginning to copy our methods of indirect fire.

> (i.) A captured graph was very nearly a facsimile of the clearance graph used in one of our Armies, but it appeared to contemplate the putting on of elevation by some form of tangent sight method.

> (ii.) Prisoners captured in the beginning of November state that "Barrage and Indirect fire is now being taught to all men in the field as far

as possible. One man from each Machine Gun Company is being sent to the *Deutsche Gewehr Fabrik*, at Spandau, for a course including instruction in Machine Gun construction and in Barrage and Indirect fire."

(*b*) In Flanders, during the month of October the enemy changed his defensive dispositions in a way which very closely affected the tactical employment of Machine Guns on both sides. Instead of the thinly held front line defended in depth by nests of Machine Guns and mazes of wire which afforded gaps through which his counter-attacking Divisions could sally, he placed more reliance on a concentration of troops in the forward area liberally supported by Machine Guns. His counter-attacks were therefore delivered much sooner than previously, and by troops much closer forward. By the end of the month he seems to have found that this change had been carried too far, and reverted to a middle policy of keeping his main counter troops well in rear, and at the same time maintaining his extra stock of fire power in the front line, especially Machine Guns. These changes affected our own Machine Gun tactics in two ways:—(i.) It increased the importance of the task assigned to the Machine Guns sent forward to consolidate in the neighbourhood of the final objective. (ii.) It made an *immediate* response to S.O.S. calls of critical importance.

The effect of the Machine Gun Barrage, as reported by prisoners, under the latest tactical conditions may be estimated from the following extracts:—

"Our Machine Gun Barrage was so effective on October 30th, that reinforcements were entirely cut off. Several attempts were made to get through, but proved unsuccessful on account of the heavy fire of our Machine Guns.

"The 22nd Bav. Inf. Regt. were entirely cut off from their reserves by our Machine Gun fire. Both the front line and reserve Companies sustained very heavy casualties, and the men in the front line, seeing that they could not expect any reinforcements, surrendered." (Second Army Summary of November 2.)

On the subject of Intelligence the Second Army report makes the following recommendation:—" The Machine Gun Company being a single unit distributed over a Brigade front and in close touch with Brigade H.Q., has opportunities for collecting information greater than those possessed by any Infantry Battalion. Section Officers and N.C.O.s should be trained in what to report and how to report it. Opportunities might be taken during winter months of attaching Officers and N.C.O.s of the Machine Gun Corps to the Intelligence Branch of the Staff for this purpose."

3. Forward Guns for consolidation.

The lessons emphasised in the Army Reports may be divided into two groups according as they deal with Forward or Rear guns:—

"The striking feature throughout these operations has been the execution done by Machine Guns pushed well forward—usually by guns close to the final objective. Excellent targets have been obtained, both as the enemy were retreating and when they counter-attacked. Enemy Machine Guns and strong points have been engaged and defensive flanks have been formed. Good results have been obtained both at the intermediate and final objectives; and the rôle of these guns has not been merely a defensive one. On the 20th September on one Corps front 10 to 12 guns' went forward in connection with each attacking Brigade. About 4 guns were in most cases allotted to the final objective, the remainder consolidating in depth. In view of the results obtained, the casualties were not excessive. Those actually incurred on the day of attack were in many cases slight. Some 30 casualties and the loss of two or three guns may be taken as an average for a company on the day of attack and the two following days." (Second Army.)

"To hold a Brigade front it was found that eight guns sent forward with the attacking waves were probably more than sufficient." (First Army).

In the operations at Polygon Wood, September 26/30,

the 88 Machine Guns available to support the attack of one Division were distributed as follows :—

Mobile Guns	16
Mobile Reserve Guns ...	16
Barrage Guns, Creeping ...	24
Barrage Guns, S.O.S. ...	32

The Mobile Guns were under orders "closely to support the attack of their respective Brigades."

The Mobile Reserve Guns were under the control of the G.O.C.s of Assaulting Brigades.

"The number of Mobile Guns, 8, allotted to each Brigade proved quite sufficient, even in the case of the 15th Brigade where heavy calls were made on the Machine Guns to cover the exposed flank . . . Not less than six men per gun should be sent forward with Mobile Guns. These men should all be Machine Gunners and not attached men." (Report by D.M.G.O.)

The object of Forward or Mobile Guns is to effect consolidation in depth: the guns coming into position after each objective has been definitely captured by the Infantry, and being thinned out where possible in the Intermediate objectives after the final objective has been sufficiently organized for defence.

On September 20/22 at Langemarck Ridge the work of defence was organized as follows:—

(a) "No guns were actually attached to the Infantry at all, but given certain objectives to go to in the ground captured by each Battalion, and were given strict orders to work in close co-operation with the Battalion.

(b) "The teams trained specially with the Infantry whose advance they were to support. A miniature board model was made, shewing the whole ground to be taken, the objectives of each Battalion, and of other gun-groups, the approximate direction in which they would fire when in position, and the Artillery Barrage . . . Every N.C.O. and man, both Machine Gunners and Carriers, knew as much of the scheme as the officer did before going over, and this proved invaluable, especially in the cases when the officer was wounded early in the attack.

"N.C.O.s carried on and went straight to their objectives, having a full knowledge of what their teams had to accomplish.

(c) The group of 6 guns which had been detailed to go forward for the defence of Wurst Farm area (which was in the neighbourhood of the final objective and the tactical key to the whole situation), picked their way without loss through the Artillery barrage with the exception of one gun team which went astray. On arrival the guns were established in their pre-arranged positions. "Infantry Officers were informed of the positions of these guns, and the M.G.O. endeavoured to assist in the organization of their Lewis Guns for counter-attack defence, as the orders were that this position was to be held at all costs: Wurst Farm Area being the key to everything. Eventually, by 12.30 p.m. the whole ground around this stronghold could be swept by Machine Gun, Lewis and Rifle fire.

"No gun, Vickers or Lewis, had a field of fire of less than 600 yards. The co-operation between these guns, and their excellent field of fire, proved later, in the counter-attacks, to be invaluable. Every gun, Lewis and Vickers, had a clear and specific portion of ground to cover, which minimised the amount of ammunition that might be wasted (such as would be caused by the Vickers and two Lewis firing on the same point)."

In the operations by a Division at Wallemolen at the foot of the Passchendaele Ridge, October 26th and 30th, all four Machine Gun Companies, in accordance with an earlier Divisional instruction, received their orders from the D.M.G.O., who also had the supervision of all Machine Gun training. The Forward Guns came under the orders of the Group Commander of the Rear Guns at advanced Brigade Headquarters. This arrangement was made with a view to co-ordinating the work of Forward and Rear Guns and keeping the D.M.G.O. in immediate touch with the general Machine Gun situation. Thus, when two guns of the Right consolidating section were hit by shell fire, they were promptly replaced from the Barrage Batteries which in

turn received guns from the rear. On October 26th the casualties were very heavy, and therefore on October 30th the gun teams were under orders to proceed more slowly with their guns wrapped in water-proof sheets. The casualties were then very light, and "as soon as the Infantry line was established, the whole front was covered by the cross-fire of these guns." Their orders were:—
"These sections will advance after reconnaissance by bounds of about 50 yards. They will take every precaution to keep their guns and belt-boxes clean. Their duty is to deal with counter-attacks in force and not with snipers and small parties which will be dealt with by riflemen or Lewis Guns of Battalions."

4. Rear Guns for covering the advance, and S.O.S.

In contrast with the advance attempted on July 31st, the advances made by the Infantry in the latter stages of the Ypres operations were much shorter. This materially affected the tactics of the Rear Guns and enabled them to take steps for surmounting difficulties which had been experienced in the earlier stages.

"The shortness of range of a Machine Gun barrage makes it difficult to select positions clear of the hostile Artillery barrage. In consequence, barrage Machine Guns are very liable to be silenced, and it has been found in operations on a large scale, Machine Gun barrages soon become thin and patchy." (First Army.)

"The failure of Machine Guns to be able to deliver effective barrage fire in certain operations has been invariably traced to the difficulties in re-loading wet belts by hand (the employment of the existing type of belt-loading machines being altogether out of the question) and the lack of ammunition in dry belts." (Second Army.)

To give the fullest value and the greatest reliability to the Machine Gun. barrage under the exceptionally difficult fighting conditions in the Ypres theatre, various expedients have been adopted.

In the case of one Division, dumps of S.A.A. and strong weather-proof belt-filling shelters were erected in the forward area during the comparatively quiet period before the Divisional relief; and on the night following the firing of the barrage, by which time the objective had been fully organized for defence, the barrage guns were very considerably thinned out.

In other cases higher rates of fire than usual, *e.g.*, 100 rounds per minute for 1 hour 40 minutes, and wider traverses were adopted. "In a programme shoot in shelled areas guns should not be called on to fire at a less rate than 75 rounds per minute. To fire at a slower rate involves the exposure of more guns and teams than is necessary. All available guns should be mounted at the conclusion of the shoot for the S.O.S." (First Army.)

Nearly all reports of operations emphasise the importance of avoiding, when possible, the necessity for a forward move of the barrage batteries, for two reasons :—

(i.) The exposure to shell fire while moving.
(ii.) The difficulty of carrying up sufficient S.A.A. to a forward position for S.O.S. work.

In contrast with Vimy and Messines, where a continuous covering barrage was considered necessary, it has now become more usual to put the Machine Gun barrage on selected parts of the front only. The chief reason for this has been the exceptional density of our own Artillery barrage in the Ypres sector, and the small depth of advance attempted on any one day. For example, on September 26th, at 'Sgrafenstafel, the 64 guns of one Division were divided into :—

Rear guns	40
Forward or Mobile guns ...	24
Total	64

Instead of a continuous barrage the guns fired by batteries on (i.) "Pill-box" areas, (ii.) the 'Sgrafenstafel cross-roads, (iii.) along the Hannebeke valley. They had also as their second task a final S.O.S. line 400 yards ahead of the Infantry objective.

The covering fire, beginning at Zero or later, was maintained for two hours after the arrival of the Infantry at the final objectives, which were consolidated without interference from the enemy.

The S.O.S. barrage line was on the basis of 30 yards per gun, and when called for at 3.15 p.m. it was down before the Artillery barrage.

On September 26th, at Polygon Wood, another Division adopted a further modification. Each of the two groups of Rear guns had a separate task. The creeping barrage group (Right) covered the Infantry advance to the intermediate Red line, firing 50 rounds per minute. It was then under orders to "Stand by until ordered to withdraw"; but the attack of the Division on its right partially failed, and therefore batteries of this group were switched to assist the arrested advance by area shooting. "They were instrumental in breaking up counter-attacks on more than one occasion, and on the 27th opened fire on seven different occasions in the British area. At 4.30 p.m. on the 27th these guns were firing on localities where the enemy were reported to be massing for attack, one minute and ten seconds after the information reached me" (Report by D.M.G.O.). Constant telephonic communication was maintained between D.M.G.O. and the creeping barrage group. The guns were in position for 60 hours.

The S.O.S. Rear group was allotted the task of replying to S.O.S. calls on an S.O.S. line 500 yards ahead of the final objective. In addition, during the consolidation of this line it searched its frontage to a depth of 800 yards. Between 7.30 a.m. of September 26th and 11.55 p.m. on September 28th, ten S.O.S. calls were answered, at a total expenditure of 738,000 rounds (including 314,000 for the first call on September 26th). The guns were in position for 85 hours. After 8.45 a.m. on September 26th, all communication with the S.O.S. group was by runners, as the buried cable was cut. This, however, did not interfere with their work. "These guns are usually firing for many minutes before word can be sent to the Group Commander even when communication holds."

The above arrangement suggests a very interesting point. It is of course open to the objection, noted in the

Second Army report, that two sets of positions have to be dug, and two sets of men have to be kept under fire during operations. But where there is a choice of ground and good cover in positions which would not be suitable for S.O.S. work, it is possible that batteries here can fulfil a double function. They can take part in covering the initial advance; and also, because, being on less exposed ground they can hope to maintain telephonic communication, they can be used as switch batteries for concentrated fire on areas opposite their own front or that of an adjacent Division.

The extent to which observation can be obtained varies with the weather and the position which the Battery or Group occupies with reference to the operations as a whole. On the flank in clear weather, as for example at the capture of Hill 70, north of Lens, in August last, it was possible to direct the fire of a group of batteries in a Division covering the Canadian left flank from an observation post on commanding ground. It is also on the flank of an attack where the Infantry advance is small or nil, that telephonic communication can be most easily maintained. It is, however, sometimes possible to get good observation even in the centre of an attack. Thus, on September 20th from Shrewsbury Forest it was possible to observe not only enemy movements, but also the strike of the bullets on the ground (the ground being dry and the concentration of fire intense). The Rear guns here, which were divided as usual into two groups right and left, were sufficiently under control to enable one group to co-operate with the other when there was a check on the latter's front.

The Battery positions had been selected as far forward as possible with a view to avoiding a forward move. In addition to covering the Infantry advance and firing on the S.O.S. line during the main counter-attack later in the day, the Batteries, by reason of having good observation and communication, were able to fire on several different occasions on enemy troops as they were preparing for the counter-attack. In this way Machine Gun fire could be directed on to enemy targets from Zero hour right down to and including the main counter-attack.

5. Forward and Rear Guns.

Hitherto the term Mobile Gun has been applied to guns detailed for consolidation because they have to go forward before they can consolidate, and the arrangements for their move are almost the most important part of their work, but it would be a mistake to suppose that Forward or Mobile Guns are in any sense peculiarly appropriate to Mobile warfare. The contrary is the case. These guns are only intended to come into action when a position has been won and the fighting is momentarily stationary. While they are fulfilling their normal rôle they are not helping to cover the Infantry advance. Moreover, inasmuch as when the Infantry are moving the guns also are moving at some distance behind, they are apt to be caught at a tactical disadvantage if they are hurried up into action suddenly. It is therefore to be anticipated that just as the stationary barrage guns cover the advance in warfare against highly organized defences when the total move is a small one, so some form of barrage guns of the nature of Mobile Batteries will be required to follow up and support by overhead fire the several successive stages of a more or less continuous advance. It is therefore possible that more instruction will be obtained from a study of the arrangements at the earlier fighting at Vimy and Messines than from the subsequent and perhaps exceptional type of warfare now under consideration.

6. S.O.S. Barrage in Defence.

The report of the Division referred to on the operation of September 26th submits as the final tactical lesson, "The advisability of considering Machine Gun S.O.S. Barrage a permanent portion of all defensive schemes, owing to the *rapidity* with which such Machine Guns can open fire." This is in accordance with the suggestion put forward in previous *résumés*. Central control, flexibility and rapidity of action are the three great desiderata of Machine Gun barrage fire, and the operations of the third battle of Ypres have supplied a most valuable training ground for the realisation of these lessons in the most trying conditions.

7. Lessons.

The principal lessons to be learnt from the operations under review may be summarised as follows:—

(a) The Germans are undoubtedly very much impressed by the effectiveness of our present methods of employing Machine Guns, and we may expect a gradual development on similar lines in the German army.

The normal German establishment is now:—

Light Machine Guns: 2–3 per infantry company. (72–108 per division.)

Heavy Machine Guns: 8–12 per battalion machine gun company. (72–108 per division.)

The minimum figure is probably normal for divisions in quiet sectors of the front, the maximum being reached in active sectors.

The average number per division is:—

90 light Machine Guns
90 heavy ,,   ,,

Total 180

There are also about 90 independent Machine Gun "marksman" detachments (each of 3 companies), which are G.H.Q. troops and are allotted as required to particular sectors of the front. These companies are similar in establishment to the battalion Machine Gun Companies. Any development of scientific Machine Gunnery by the enemy, therefore, is deserving of the most serious consideration and can only be met by still further scientific development on our part.

The development of rapidly produced Barrage Fire by organized Machine Gun Batteries will be an essential feature of any successful effort at pushing forward under conditions of open warfare to exploit an initial success, when adequate Field Artillery Support is lacking.

For this reason, it must be realised that the development of scientific Machine Gunnery is as important from an open or semi-open warfare point of view, as it is from a trench warfare point of view, and this should be very carefully considered in the winter training of all Machine Gun Companies.

(b) There is still a tendency to push forward too many Forward Guns into the forward portions of the positions to be consolidated.

(c) The fact that the Forward Guns should work on as carefully a thought out plan, and be given as definite orders, as the Rear Guns, still wants further emphasising.

(d) Forward Guns should seldom be definitely attached to Infantry Battalions; they should have definite orders as to routes, positions, etc., and be directly under the Brigade to which they have been allotted. The Machine Gun Commander at Brigade Headquarters should also be the channel of communication between the Brigade Commander and the Forward Guns.

(e) The great importance of an efficient Machine Gun S.O.S. Barrage has again been brought out, and the necessity of the Machine Gun Barrage being "flexible" and easy of control has been demonstrated on many occasions.

(f) There still appears a tendency in some Divisions to use Machine Guns for work that is essentially the rôle of Riflemen or Lewis Guns, namely, to deal with snipers, infiltration, and early small local counter-attacks.

The tendency is dangerous insomuch as it weakens the Machine Gun defence in depth against the larger counter-attacks which develop later.

———

NOTE.—It is clear that the terms "Mobile Guns" and "Barrage Guns" hitherto used are misleading. It has therefore been decided to adopt the following:—

Forward Guns, that is, the guns allotted to Infantry Brigades to go forward in support of the attacking Battalions and carry out consolidation in depth of the ground won.

Rear Guns, that is the guns which supply barrage and other forms of covering fire from positions in rear.

S.S. 201. O.B./2007.

(Not to be taken into Action or Front Line Trenches.)

TACTICAL SUMMARY of MACHINE GUN OPERATIONS

No. 2. NOVEMBER—DECEMBER 1917

FOR OFFICIAL USE ONLY.

This Document is the property of H.B.M. Government, and the information in it is not to be communicated, either directly or indirectly, to the Press or any person not holding an official position in His Majesty's Service.

[ISSUED BY THE GENERAL STAFF.]

The present Summary covers two months, and is divided into:—

Part I.—Concluding stages of the operations North-East of Ypres

Part II.—The battle of Cambrai.

S,S. 201.] [O.B./2007.

Tactical Summary of Machine Gun Operations for November and December, 1917.

PART I.—CONCLUDING STAGES OF THE OPERATIONS N.E. OF YPRES.

1.—Forward Guns.

The necessity is again emphasized for the following:
(a) Studied economy in the handling of the forward guns;
(b) intimate knowledge of Infantry tactics and the actual dispositions of the Infantry; (c) co-ordination with the Lewis Guns.

(a) Economy is obtained by using the fire power of these guns from the most opportune ground and getting them to and from that ground with a minimum of loss. Thus:—

(i.) " When ground permits, it has been demonstrated that forward guns can assist the advance of the Infantry more by bringing to bear direct overhead fire than by advancing with the Infantry." (First Army, November.)

(ii.) " The advance should be carried out by bounds, the gun teams moving in formations suitable to the prevailing conditions " (*i.e.*, the principle of the bound is a constant one, but its application varies according as the advance is over water-logged shell holes, as at Ypres, over deep and undestroyed trenches, as at Cambrai, over woodland or open country). . . . To quote one example of an advance over a shell area, " the teams advanced in files by bounds, the sub-section officer leading. A small interval was observed between files. The officer went forward and decided the limit of each bound; he then gave the teams who were taking cover in shell holes the signal to advance."

(iii.) " The relief of guns which have gone forward with an attack may be facilitated in many cases by attaching a liaison officer from the relieving company to the H.Q. of the attacking company." (Second Army, November.)

(b) and (c) are different aspects of the same problem, viz., co-operation between Machine Guns and Infantry.

"In training, more instructions might be given to Officers and N.C.O.s regarding the assistance to the Infantry in attacking strong points which are holding up the advance. This should be done:—

"(i.) By bringing frontal fire to bear upon the obstacle while the Infantry make flanking attacks.

"(ii.) By bringing fire to bear from the flanks while the Infantry attack from the front." (First Army, November.)

The Lewis Gun is the natural link between the Vickers Gun and the Infantry, and it is impossible to know whether both types of automatic weapon are being correctly and fully employed, unless their effort is regarded as a joint one. Co-operation is not always easy, but in one Corps of the Second Army (which in its October report recommended the attachment of Lewis Gunners for a time to their Brigade Machine Gun Company) the following cases are quoted, and it will be seen that they correspond with the needs noted by the First Army:—

(i.) Vickers Guns kept up overhead frontal fire upon an enemy strong point, while the Lewis Guns crept to a flank and assisted the Infantry to take the position. The Vickers Gun was firing from a slight rise (a ruined house)." Also, "Vickers Guns occupied the main line of the objective, while Lewis Guns were thrown slightly forward on the flanks." This corresponds to (i.) above.

"Lewis Guns were made responsible for the immediate front of the objective, while Vickers Guns covered the flanks and more distant approaches." This corresponds to (ii.) above.

2.—Rear Guns.

It is even more true of the rear guns than of the forward guns that the majority of losses may be incurred after the attack and initial consolidation, when they are kept in the same positions for several days in readiness for S.O.S. calls.

At the end of October one Division worked under the following arrangements with uniform success:—"After dawn on Z plus 1 day, provided no large enemy counter-attacks had developed, rear guns, with the exception of two sections, each of four guns, were withdrawn. These sections were prepared to put down a switch barrage on whatever portion of the front might be counter-attacked. As a result, the Machine Gunners were not unduly fatigued, there were few cases of sickness or trench feet, and the men after a few days' rest were ready for another battle." It is therefore considered that "after an attack the number of rear guns could normally be reduced on a Divisional front. These should be given 'S.O.S.' lines in front of particularly dangerous points and should also carry out harassing fire at night."

This arrangement clearly premised barrage flexibility, which depends, of course, on communications and training, but it must also be interpreted with reference to the very exceptional conditions prevailing at Ypres. The enemy's main strength was in his forward system, his Machine Guns were in pill-boxes sometimes right in front, his counter-attacking troops not very far behind, and the ground was so sodden that he could not concentrate from a distance. Indeed, provided that he, or the mud, had imposed on us a sufficient delay, he frequently had no motive for attempting to regain the few hundred yards of ground lost, in case his immediate counter-attacks failed.

In drier conditions, and on ground which the enemy regards as vital to his battle zone, it would be unsafe to thin out the rear guns so quickly and so considerably; and although the sites of certain guns and the personnel of the companies ought no doubt to be changed as soon as opportunity allows, the ultimate disposition required by the ground may be a stronger and more continuous screen of long-distance Machine Gun fire than has been possible either during or immediately after consolidation. In fact, the conditions may then change from the principles of offence to those of defence, *i.e.*, when the maximum use of Machine Guns should be made in order to thin out the infantry holding the position.

3.—Reserve Guns.

Normally, some guns should be kept " in reserve and reorganizing." But in protracted operations, such as those in Flanders, it was not always possible to maintain a regular percentage in transport lines definitely outside the battlefield. The question rather was, " Shall there be a distinct mobile reserve earmarked for the forward guns, or simply a single reserve under the control of the D.M.G.O. ? "

On this experience differs. One Division, which at Polygon Wood, September 26th, had replenished its forward guns from its creeping barrage group, found that this did not work well, and that it was better to keep half its forward guns in reserve and leave the barrage group intact. But the Corps to which this Division belonged, when operating near Passchendaele early in November, reported that the forward guns had suffered severe losses and were of little use, and therefore recommended that only a small proportion should be sent to the final objective, the remainder being used for overhead fire from intermediate positions, and being so sited that they could put down in case of emergency short range bands of fire.

Another Division, on the other hand, in the same area found that the single reserve (*i.e.*, the rear guns feeding the forward guns and replenishing themselves from the reserve) worked well, and had the advantage of keeping the D.M.G.O. in close touch with the forward guns, and of enabling him to ascertain much more quickly their whereabouts and needs.

Whether on the actual day of attack there should be a distinct reserve will depend on a number of considerations, such as, whether the previous training and the handling during the operations are on a Divisional basis, what number of guns have been definitely allotted to Brigades, the depth of the advance, etc. In a big advance, when the batteries themselves move, it would be difficult to replenish one set of moving guns from a second. But one thing is clear. It is becoming more and more necessary, in the interest both of economy and fire effect, to have in the intermediate system as few guns as possible which are allotted for close defence only. In conditions like those at Ypres, where there was continuous heavy shelling of the intermediate areas, it is wasteful to site a large number of guns for passive defence. They do not escape loss merely by silence. There must, however, be defence in depth, and therefore the most economical solution is one which allots to the guns in rear and intermediate positions a double task—namely, to fire at long range (direct or indirect) on S.O.S. lines, and direct at short range for close defence.

4.—Centralization of Resources.

When the avenues of approach to the front system are few, long and difficult, and when the fighting is intense—that is, when constant supplies of men, guns and ammunition have to be taken over difficult country—the advantage of an organization in which Machine Gun resources are pooled, and therefore fluid, is most apparent.

The report of the Corps which on November 6th captured Passchendaele Village emphasized the following:—

Transport and Supplies.—Throughout the operations from the beginning of October to the middle of November, and in the face of heavy losses, " thanks to the fluidity of resources obtained through grouping all Machine Gun Companies in Battalions, the Machine Gun Batteries were kept in continuous being," with only two short interruptions. The forward guns, which experienced heavy casualties, were promptly reinforced. Estimated casualty wires and reports of stores destroyed were sent by D.M.G.O.s to the C.M.G.O. and promptly dealt with. The transport was effected by Battalion Pack-trains and the Motor Machine Gun Brigade, which, besides supplying batteries in each attack, transported 30 Officers, 800 O.R., Lewis Guns, Vickers Guns and stores to the scene of operations. Reinforcements were pooled, with the result that they could be posted to the units which were in the line at the time of their actual arrival. The Pack-trains, under the charge of Officers responsible for the maintenance of forward guns, brought up eight million rounds " under indescribable conditions." In this connection the present arrangement of supplying Machine Guns with ammunition in clips, as used by riflemen, is wasteful in men and material, because it necessitates the employment of six men per gun in belt filling at or near the guns, and causes movement which gives away the battery position, however well they are camouflaged. A suggestion has been made that Machine Gun ammunition should be specially packed in cheap cotton or paper belts, which would be used only once (this overcomes the problem of wet belts), and be brought up in special boxes, each containing two belts of 250 rounds. This matter is receiving attention.

Communications, Liaison and Control.—(i.) " In active sectors air lines are a snare, and attempts to maintain them are responsible for too many casualties. Some form of visual signalling, or . . . rockets will have to be adopted. A clear line (in buried cable) between the O.C. Machine Guns at Brigade Headquarters and O.C. Rear Machine Gun Group is essential."

(ii.) During the concluding phase Divisions detailed a Forward Liaison Officer, whose duty it was to check the location of the Forward Guns and see that correct liaison was established by them with the adjoining Infantry Battalions. This worked well; on November 6th the location of all Forward Machine Guns was correctly reported by noon.

Two examples are given of forward Machine Gun officers taking command of Infantry Companies in an emergency; and from these and other cases it is considered that there is no justification for the " fears expressed from time to time that as a result of a higher organization the Machine Gunners might become estranged from the Infantry."

(iii.) A new method of tactical organization was tried in one Division and found very successful, and the report recommends that it should be adopted throughout the Corps during future operations. The method is as follows:—
" The Machine Guns situated in a Brigade area were divided into two groups: Forward Groups including Consolidating Guns and Sniping Batteries, and Rear Groups including all the batteries covering the front of the Brigade.

" These Groups were placed respectively under an O.C. Forward Group and an O.C. Rear Group. These O.sC. Forward and Rear Groups were placed, the first on the buried cable at the point nearest to the Barrage Batteries, and the other at the Headquarters of a Battalion connected to the Brigade at Headquarters.

" A Senior Machine Gun Officer was at Brigade Headquarters, and the Brigadier exercised the command and control of all the guns placed under him through this Officer. . . ."

Thus, " the Brigadier has at his disposal, to exercise command and control of the Machine Guns, a Senior Officer who is conversant with the situation both as to Forward Guns and Rear Batteries. So as to maintain the personal touch, the Senior Machine Gun Officer at Brigade Headquarters should be as far as possible the Officer Commanding the Machine Gun Company previously affiliated to the Brigade." (Extracts from Corps Report.)

The above considerations are of special interest in view of the fact that a Battalion organization for Machine Guns is now being adopted generally.

5.—Anti-Aircraft.

(a) At Passchendaele, and also at Cambrai, low-flying aeroplanes, in addition to their usual *rôle* of spotting positions, have harassed the movement and work of Infantry and Machine Gunners to an ever increasing extent. The trend of the enemy's tactics and the thoroughness with which they are being thought out may be gauged from the following extracts from documents captured during the summer of 1917:—

>   (i.) 17-6-17. Field Batteries must support Infantry contact aeroplanes by keeping down the fire of enemy Machine Guns, one battery registering on known Machine Gun emplacements, another taking on special targets.
>
>   (ii.) 12-6-17. The first task of Machine Guns in rear is to protect the Artillery against low-flying aeroplanes.
>
>   (iii.) 26-7-17. Special flights will precede the Infantry assault to stimulate the offensive spirit, and break down the enemy's resistance, by dropping bombs and firing Machine Guns on the heads of his Infantry. Thus, in (i.) the Artillery, by dealing with Machine Guns, facilitates the work of contact aeroplanes; in (ii.), Machine Guns protect the Artillery against hostile craft; in (iii.), aeroplanes are the eyes and forward stroke of the assault.

(b) Our own most recent experience is as follows:—

>   (i.) Passchendaele. " Low-flying aeroplanes would cruise over the area occupied by Machine

Gun Rear Batteries until some battery was spotted. Coloured lights were then dropped and a few ranging shots, observed by the aeroplane, were fired.

As soon as the range was obtained, and this was done as a rule in very few minutes, the Machine Gun Battery, or rather the area where the Battery was located, was subjected to a sudden and extremely heavy concentrated shoot by several batteries.

In some cases, when the Machine Gun Batteries realised that their positions were being registered, they tried to move to alternative positions. While moving, the personnel of these Batteries was fired at by Machine Guns from hostile aeroplanes.

(ii.) Cambrai. A special report by one Divisional Commander on the enemy's tactics on November 28th and on November 30th during his big counter-attack east of Epehy notes that the enemy aeroplanes on November 30th were "flying very low in two lines, one behind the other, each consisting of about 10 aeroplanes. The leading line swooped at the trenches, firing their Machine Guns, then opened out to the flanks, and formed up again behind the second line, which swooped and fired in its turn. The first line then came into action again, and so on."

(c) *Remedies.*

(i.) The troops themselves must be responsible for their own protection. Neither our own aeroplanes nor our anti-aircraft guns can deal satisfactorily with the low-flying enemy aeroplane.

(ii.) A new anti-aircraft sight and mounting is now being introduced.

(iii.) In every group or battery of Machine Guns, one or more guns should be equipped with anti-aircraft sights and mountings, and specially detailed for anti-aircraft protection.

(iv.) As far as possible Rear Machine Gun Batteries should be carefully camouflaged. The guns should be placed in deep, narrow slits, and all movement reduced to a minimum.

PART II.—THE BATTLE OF CAMBRAI.

1.—The Attack in the Centre and on the South.

The preliminary instruction issued by one Corps laid down that:—"Brigades attacking will require the whole of their Machine Gun Companies for the purpose of consolidation. . . " This policy had its drawbacks: in particular, it diminished the chance of effective covering fire from Machine Guns on occasions when, in the partial or temporary absence of Artillery support, such Machine Gun fire was especially needed. Several sections of Machine Guns, which were for a short time employed in giving direct covering fire over the canal, are reported to have done very valuable work. "On one occasion two sections were employed together, and the effect of this concentration of fire was most successful." (Fourth Army, December.) One Division had arranged the firing of the second phase of the barrage from their second positions for a time which hardly gave the guns a chance of getting up. Batteries, however, had been informed beforehand of this, and the advantage of the arrangement was that if the Infantry advance had been held up the guns would have been well in hand and in a position to give concentrated covering fire.

In getting forward their difficulties were of the following order:—

(i.) *Uncut wire and unbridged trenches.*—The Tank tracks could not be made use of for the Pack-train, as the wire was trampled and not cut and was dangerous for the mules.

(ii.) *Enemy Snipers and Machine Guns.*—In a surprise advance of this nature, when the Infantry must push on quickly, there is a greater likelihood of pockets of the enemy being overlooked, and there is, therefore, as great a need of careful scouting by the Rear Guns, as they move forward, as by the Forward Guns. In a Division operating on the North insufficient reconnaissance led to the surprise of one Battery just as it was coming into action.

2.—The Attack on the North.

The Machine Guns working with the Brigade of the Division which had the task of working up the Hindenburg system made full preparations for covering fire, but the following difficulties are noted in the report of the D.M.G.O.:—

> (i.) The D.M.G.O. was up with his Battery and "found it very difficult to get communication with Division. . . A capable and experienced officer, and perhaps a second officer to assist, should be detailed to maintain the supply of ammunition, rations, water, etc.: there was shortage in the first two days of S.A.A. and the men were without supplies."
>
> (ii.) The first forward move of the batteries took them to a slag heap, where it was intended to fire on the retiring enemy, but it was found "impossible to open fire owing to the consistent uncertainty of the position of our own Infantry."
>
> (iii.) Signalling communications were faulty, the absence of a Signalling Officer being specially felt, and liaison with the Infantry was found hard to maintain. "Infantry do not ask Machine Gun Batteries to co-operate with them or protect them, and often valuable time is lost before it is possible to find their exact location."

As regards the action of the Forward Guns, the following opinion is expressed:—"The officers in command of Forward Guns did not know their *rôle*, and were always too far behind the Infantry. They were certainly not used with any boldness, and they missed many good opportunities on the first two days of the operations." (Report by D.M.G.O.) This criticism raises the important question—what is the primary *rôle* of the Forward Guns in the first 24 or 48 hours of an attack of this nature? The answer, "consolidation in readiness for the set-piece attacks which will come later," rather assumes that the main tactical idea will not be realized. Secondly, in a surprise attack exceptional opportunities do occur of good Machine Gun targets on a retreating enemy. Finally, when the enemy himself made his big attack on November 30th, his Machine Guns followed it up with exceptional speed. By the same evening he had lined his flank on the high ground S. of Villers-Guislain with Machine Guns (a part no doubt being light Machine Guns). Similarly, when a small piece of commanding ground taken by the enemy on November 30th was recaptured from him the next day, 50 prisoners and no fewer than 17 Machine Guns were taken.

In order to give a satisfactory answer, it is necessary to consider automatic fire power as a whole and to distinguish between the different purposes for which it is required in the forward system. It is required:—

(a) To assist the Infantry in clearing out enemy parties and in silencing snipers and individual Machine Guns. This is the work of the Lewis Guns.

(b) To organize for defence the ground won. This is the work of the Lewis Guns and Vickers Guns together, the Vickers Guns being reserved for the organization of the most important features, and not necessarily defending those features by being placed on them. Whether a Vickers Gun should be sent to the final objective depends on whether that is *the* critical feature, and whether it is best defended by guns placed in it or just in rear or to the flank. When a further advance is contemplated immediately, the advantage of defending features which, though tactically important, do not themselves necessarily give commanding observation (*e.g.*, a wood or village) from guns just in rear, is that they will be able to fulfil a double function,—to repel a counter-attack and prevent envelopment, should a counter-attack be made, and to give covering fire in the event of a further advance.

(c) To engage enemy targets *during* the advance. For this purpose it is advantageous to have some guns (guns of opportunity) specially detailed, which have no definite responsibilities in organization, and which can therefore move where they please in search of targets. Their fire must always be observed fire, and their targets in particular should be: (1) Considerable enemy parties. (2) Nests of enemy Machine Guns. (3) Hostile low-flying aircraft. This is the work of Vickers Guns, in combination with Lewis Guns as regards the last task. In the case of the Division under consideration, it is possible that the forward Machine Guns might have discharged their tasks more effectively if they had been separated more definitely on the lines suggested.

3.—General Lessons of the Attack.

The Machine Gun lessons learnt during the period of attack may be summarised as follows:—

(a) The more open the fighting becomes, the more necessary is it that a large number of Machine Guns be retained under the hand of the Commander of the Force for the purposes of covering the advance. These guns organized in mobile batteries will form:—

    (i.) A strong rear line of defence in case of a reverse.

    (ii.) A reserve of fire power in the hand of the Commander, available to assist in exploiting a success.

(b) It is essential to the success of an advance where the available Artillery support is for a time limited, that the arrangements made for supporting the Infantry advance with Machine Gun fire from positions in rear should be definite and thorough.

(c) The D.M.G.O. should not personally command a Group of Machine Gun Batteries. He should keep in close touch with the General Staff of his Division, see to the arrangements for supply to Batteries of S.A.A., etc., and be in readiness to direct any reorganization necessary to meet a change of circumstances.

4. The holding attack at Bullecourt was very successful from a Machine Gun point of view:—

"Neutralizing fire. During the operations on November 20th, a German machine gunner was captured who stated that our Machine Gun fire in the neighbourhood of Fontaine-les-Croiselles was so intense that four Machine Guns were unable to come into action, and the teams remained in their dug-outs during the attack. The value of grouping Machine Guns into Batteries to support an attack and protect the Infantry during and after organization of the ground gained has been emphasized once more. All counter-attacks were broken up." (Third Army, November.)

5.—Wood Fighting.

(a) In the Division which captured Bourlon Wood on November 23rd, it had been decided that "the main *rôle* of the guns would be one of overhead barrage fire, and protection of the flanks in case the attacks of the Divisions E. and W. failed. This protection of the flanks proved to be of inestimable value." (Report by D.M.G.O.) Accordingly, each Brigade sent forward four guns for consolidation, keeping 12 for barrage and flank protection. When Bourlon Village was not taken, the forward guns were withdrawn, and rejoined the barrage groups.

(b) No guns were put in Bourlon Wood—a policy which was not followed later. Doubtless a big wooded area is capable of being strongly organized for defence by Machine Guns, but while the situation is fluctuating and the hold on the wood is precarious, Machine Guns will in general be better employed in covering the flanks and exits. On November 23rd eight Machine Guns of the Right Brigade Company of the attacking Division were placed on the eastern edge to form a belt of fire along the side of it. Though on the extremity of the wood, " these guns did excellent work. Five successive counter-attacks were made by the Germans in one day (November 24th) on this flank. These were beaten off before they reached our lines; the other two succeeded in reaching and penetrating our front position, but were immediately afterwards driven back. Of the eight guns, only two were put out of action.

" All guns had excellent targets at the enemy assembling for the attack at a range of about 1,000 yards, and also the whole time he was approaching and attacking. When guns are used in this way, they must be in pairs, and, if possible, in fours " (owing to ease of control, the greater effectiveness of the combined fire of several guns, and the moral effect of numbers and the presence of an officer).

6.—Village Fighting.

Similar lessons were learnt as regards village fighting.

(a) Machine Guns should not be crowded in villages.

(b) " It is dangerous to push Machine Guns forward into villages until they have been properly cleared." (Third Army, December.)

(c) The report by the Division which attacked Bourlon Village emphasizes the following tasks:—

      (i.) To assist clearing parties.

(ii.) To defend the rear of our foremost troops in case the clearing parties experience serious difficulty (that is, in particular, to prevent *envelopment*).

(iii.) To form islands of resistance.

" It must be recognized that in open fighting the enemy will not bombard a village while fighting is going on in or near it, that the actual situation will not be known by the enemy for some time, which will prevent still further his bombardment, and that finally an effective and an annihilating bombardment of a village in open fighting is almost impossible, or at all events would require several days. As soon as our foremost Infantry are definitely established beyond the village and the work of clearing has been completed, then, and not till then, Machine Guns may be moved to the flanks, rear, or in front of, the village as required."

These lessons were amply borne out in the attack which one Division made on Fontaine on November 27th. Their main casualties came from Machine Gun fire on the flank (La Folie Wood), and from the high ground beyond the village. More neutralizing fire by Machine Guns was needed on these places. The Forward Guns detailed to take up positions in front of the village on either flank were unable to get there. The Machine Guns detailed to occupy cross-roads in the centre of the village were held up by snipers, and took up position at the rear end. However, on the withdrawal of the Infantry, all the forward guns except two were by skilful handling successfully withdrawn.

7.—The Counter-Attack: Machine Gun Defence on the North.

(i.) The enemy attacks along Bourlon Wood were dealt with by a combination of short range and long range fire. One Brigade reports, as regards the forward guns, "All the enemy attacks on our right were dealt with in enfilade by our Machine Guns (direct fire), and their fire was a powerful factor in determining the issue of the fight on this flank." They were assisted by three forward Machine Guns of the next Brigade " dug in close to our front line. Had they been further back their fire would not have been nearly so efficient, as our men in front of them would have masked them. Their fire is reported to have been more effective than that of the

Lewis Guns, which is only to be expected, as the former are firing from a fixed platform." The Lewis Guns, on the other hand, made use of their greater mobility. " When the big rush of the enemy was at its height, several Lewis Gun detachments on their own initiative moved from positions in the line which were not being attacked, and took up other positions from where they got really fine targets which they at once took advantage of, and in this way accounted for hundreds of the enemy and drove the survivors back in confusion."

In certain cases forward guns were ultimately surrounded and cut off, but not before they had done serious execution. One reason why their fire was so effective was that the enemy, presumably because of the uncertainty of the situation, put down his barrage well behind our front line, even behind that of the Infantry supports.

(ii.) Further to the left, the nature of the country and correspondingly the type of Machine Gun defence were different. The main line of resistance commanded a long view down the Canal du Nord on to Moeuvres and the adjacent slopes. Consequently, the majority of the Machine Guns on this sector were grouped for barrage fire in the neighbourhood of the main line of resistance. One battery which had tried to take up forward positions to protect the left flank by direct fire was heavily shelled and had to withdraw. This experience shows the difficulty of grouping guns in a forward position for direct fire. On November 30th, the Group Commander of the Machine Guns was at Brigade Headquarters, and in touch not only with his Brigadier, but also with the O.C., Left Group, R.A., who had his Headquarters in the same dug-out. Therefore, he had "unique facilities for information of all movements: both Batteries being in telephonic communication by direct wire to Machine Gun Exchange, which itself had a direct wire back to Brigade Headquarters." On the morning of the 30th, the enemy was observed massing about Quarry Wood and entering Moeuvres. This was followed by a heavy bombardment and the S.O.S. call: whereupon " all guns opened rapid fire and many direct targets were obtained, as the enemy came down slopes in wave after wave. . . Throughout this day and night most excellent work was done by Batteries, and the system of controlled and co-ordinated Machine Gun fire by the Battery method was amply justified. The necessity for duplicate telephone wires was brought out, as the efficiency of the method depends largely on reliable and quick communications."

The lessons drawn by the Commander of the Machine Gun Batteries are as follows:—

> (a) The suitability of the battery system for defence, " even when there is no time to organize batteries in the most approved method, namely guns laid out in line and exact parallelism obtained."
>
> (b) The importance of communication.
>
> These, while they held, enabled the Group Commander (a) to know how each battery was progressing; (b) to get guns on to enemy concentrations without, or in advance of, the S.O.S. signal.
>
> (c) The Group Commander should be in close touch with his Brigadier and the Group Commander of the R.A., " to get information at the earliest possible moment."

The defence on the North was much strengthened by the strong Machine Gun defence provided by the Division on the left flank, which was responsible for the sector where our new and old lines joined. In addition to an S.O.S. barrage on the Hindenburg system South of Inchy, there were three lines of Machine Gun defence to stem a break through by the enemy from either the North-East or the North-West. On November 30th, telephonic communication was very good, and the D.M.G.O. at Left Group H.Q. was in touch with nearly all his guns and could move up reserve guns from the Divisional pool as required. As the result of judicious placing and no movement by day the total casualties incurred between November 19th and December 3rd (the Division was on the flank of the attack on November 20th), were under two dozen and four guns damaged. Apart from Artillery support and some Infantry posts in No Man's Land, the defence on certain parts of this flank was mainly a Machine Gun defence.

8.—Machine Gun Defence in the Centre.

On December 6th, South of Bourlon Wood, the enemy attacked in moderate strength our new positions in front of the Hindenburg Support Line.

The Division on the flank of this attack reports that " in anticipation of heavy counter-attacks by the enemy, a large number of guns were placed in the front and support line, which were situated for the main part on a crest from which the ground sloped away in a manner exceptionally favourable for direct Machine Gun fire, the enemy having to cross from 1,000 to 2,000 yards of this open ground in order to reach our trenches.

" On the afternoon of December 6th, the value of these guns was demonstrated during an attempted attack against the Division on our left (*i.e.*, to the North): large bodies of the enemy being engaged by the guns on the left sector with considerable success, the attack breaking down under combined Artillery and Machine Gun fire."

The experiences of the Machine Guns of the Division which bore the weight of this attack were as follows:—

(i.) The foremost guns got good targets, but became isolated by the Infantry's withdrawal, and in retiring suffered casualties in guns and men.

(ii.) The intermediate guns, after firing 5,000 rounds, had their fire masked by the Infantry, and then withdrew.

(iii.) The section of four guns in front of the village got good targets after the outpost line had come in. " Patrols later found lines of dead Germans who had been caught by the fire of these guns."

(iv.) The next and following nights heavy night-firing programmes were carried out—Machine Guns, Trench Mortars and Artillery dividing up the ground thus:—

Zone A.—Front line to 700 yards back. Trench Mortars, Patrols and Lewis Guns.

Zone B.—700-1,800 yards Machine Guns.

Zone C.—1,800 yards and upwards. Artillery.

The result was that " the enemy has not been able to consolidate a line within 1,000 yards of our front line." The D.M.G.O. notes among lessons learnt that " in an attack the Machine Gun Batteries are more likely to escape a hostile barrage than in defence. In the defence it is possible for the enemy to break through a thinly held outpost line and to escape the S.O.S. barrage."

This opinion should be contrasted with the experiences detailed in para. 7, especially the lessons drawn at the end of (ii.).

9.—Machine Gun Defence on the South.

The attack of November 30th on the South brought out the following points:—

(a) Any kind of linear Machine Gun defence should be avoided. The Machine Gun plan must rather aim at the defence of features of tactical importance, at closer grouping on the Battery system, the use of " switching " and direct fire against enemy troops who have penetrated deeply into the position.

(b) One method of strengthening the Machine Gun defence on a sector which has to be thinly held by Infantry is to have in reserve special Machine Gun formations, tactically billeted at points from which they can be brought up to positions previously selected and prepared, in time to arrest any serious peneration. (With reference to these special formations, " Machine Gun Marksman Detachments," in the German Army, *see* October Summary, No. 1, para. 7.)

10.—Employment of Machine Guns to Cover Withdrawal.

The way in which Machine Guns should be employed to cover a withdrawal is laid down in S.S. 192, " The Employment of Machine Guns," Part I., Sec. 44; and the experience of one Division illustrates the suitability of the procedure there laid down.

The Machine Guns in this case were employed as follows:—First of all, the rear guns from the neighbourhood of the covering line covered the withdrawal of the forward guns. Then certain of the former forward guns took up positions in the new outpost line, from where they could by direct overhead fire cover in turn the withdrawal of the guns in the covering line.

The guns engaged in these tasks were organized in four-gun batteries. During the withdrawal, as well as during the counter-attack of November 30th, it was found that this organization " gives a heavy concentration of fire which is easily controllable, and also very largely increases the steadiness of the gun teams, thus enabling fire to be withheld longer than would be the case when isolated guns were employed." But it is also stated that in rearguard actions of this nature " a definite Infantry escort should be attached to each Machine Gun Team, and a larger number of carriers than is usually necessary, otherwise gun equipment may have to be abandoned, and the capture of the gun itself risked. It is impossible for a Machine Gun Team, carrying its gun and equipment, to move as fast as retiring Infantry, and therefore the order for general retirement of a Rearguard Post should be withheld until the Machine Guns have reached their next halting place."

11.—Reorganization of Machine Gun Defence after Withdrawal.

According to the account of one Division, Intelligence Reports indicated that the enemy, who by December 9th was close to the new outpost line, was likely to make another big attack with fresh Divisions, and on December 12th the Machine Gun Defences of the readjusted Divisional Front were organized in co-ordination with the Divisions on either flank. The reorganization aimed at greater depth, and took the form of adopting the battery system as the basis of defence.

The plan consisted of two parts:—

(a) *Organization and control.*—(i.) The Divisional front was organized into Machine Gun Groups, each Group being divided into two or three batteries of 4-8 guns. The few guns sited for direct fire only were attached to the Group adjacent to them. The Batteries had S.O.S. Lines, and, in addition, were sited in depth to support each other by direct fire. Practically the whole area was covered by direct fire, special attention being paid to sweeping valleys and avenues of approach.

Battery Commanders were instructed to engage favourable direct targets when these offered, in preference to continuing on their S.O.S. line.

(NOTE.—In more than one Divisional report it is urged that where guns are sited for a double purpose the site should be selected mainly with reference to its advantageousness for direct fire.)

(ii.) Harassing fire was not allowed by day or night from the battle positions, one or more guns per Battery being detached and placed in position not less than 150 yards away for this work. Movement by day near battle positions, which were all camouflaged, was forbidden. Specially appointed " liaison " officers had the task of getting out the daily programme for the batteries allotted to them, the targets being selected in conjunction with O.C. R.A. Groups from Intelligence sources.

In addition these officers had " to reconnoitre all battery positions, and know exactly what can be done from each battery position, both by direct and indirect fire."

(iii.) The D.M.G.O. co-ordinated the whole plan. The two liaison officers (one a senior officer and the other a junior) were stationed, each of them, at a Brigade Headquarters in the line. In the event of a hostile attack being imminent or taking place, the arrangement was that the D.M.G.O. should move forward at once to the Headquarters of one of the Brigades, and from there direct the Machine Gun work.

It had been the experience of this Division that it was necessary to have central control closer up than at the Division, but that a Brigade Staff was unable to cope with more than one Machine Gun Company. The expedient adopted was found practicable owing to the fact that from the peculiar nature of the ground the two Brigade Headquarters were close together, and the one to which the D.M.G.O. was to proceed was more or less in the centre of the whole Divisional Front.

(b) *Communications.*—The batteries were connected by wire with their Groups, and the Groups with each other and with both Brigade Headquarters through a special Machine Gun Exchange. In addition there was a system of runners, and visual (Lucas Lamps) was established between each Group H.Q. and the Machine Gun Exchange and also at one or two Batteries. These arrangements were only possible through the assistance of the Divisional Signalling Companies. (Similarly, the Field Survey Company had assisted in the location of the Batteries and the construction of special fighting maps.) The report states (a) that " a special Signalling Officer has been detailed to look after the Machine Gun Signal arrangements. (b) That the personnel required to maintain the system and actually employed was 1 N.C.O. and 11 men per group (three groups in all)."

12.—Third Army Report, December.

With the experience of Cambrai specially in mind, the Third Army gives, as the main Machine Gun lessons learnt therefrom, the following:—

(i.) Great advantage was experienced from grouping Machine Guns into Batteries of four. This formation gives a heavy concentration of fire, which is easily controllable, and increases the steadiness of the gun teams.

Several times during the rearguard action large bodies of the enemy came in mass upon these Machine Gun Batteries at ranges of between 200 and 400 yards, and casualties were inflicted which would have been extremely unlikely from the same number of scattered guns.

(ii.) Indirect barrages and harassing fire were very usefully employed, but under open warfare conditions main reliance should be placed on direct fire over open sights.

(iii.) The necessity has again been emphasized of keeping Machine Guns on the flanks of each Brigade during an attack, in order to form a defensive flank in the event of units on either side being unable to get forward. These guns should advance some way behind the assaulting waves.

(iv.) Machine Guns for defence must be distributed in depth. Well organized attacks are practically certain to capture the front line, but they soon lose weight and a few Machine Guns distributed in depth can do a great deal towards holding them up completely.

In this connection the necessity for the co-ordination of Divisional Machine Gun Defence schemes has again been brought out.

The co-operation of Lewis Guns in these schemes must also be taken into account.

13.—General Summary.

The above paras. 1 to 12 may be summarised as follows:—

(a) A considerable part of the Machine Guns available must be kept in hand to provide covering fire during the later stages of the assault; and, therefore, it is essential that guns should not be split up too soon and detailed in larger numbers than is absolutely necessary to the organization for defence of the first objectives.

(b) If guns are distributed among Brigades and by them allotted to Battalions, it is very difficult in an emergency to centralise them.

(c) Other things being equal, direct fire is superior to indirect fire, and direct observation should always be sought.

But other things very often are not .equal. For in a general attack the direct close range fire of Machine Guns is apt to be masked by the advancing Infantry; and in defence it will be the object of the enemy's Artillery, at any rate on an established front, to silence in particular the front line positions from which this direct fire can be delivered.

(d) The solution lies in a balance of conflicting claims, and a good working compromise is a combination of direct and indirect fire—of indirect fire (observed where possible) on an S.O.S. line, changing into direct fire for close defence in emergency.

(e) The more vehement the anticipated attack or counter-attack of the enemy, the more the balance turns in favour of adopting a defence in depth by means of a grouped resistance on the battery system.

(f) In defence, as in attack, the success of the battery system is closely bound up with the success of communication. Divisional grouping and the assistance of the Divisional Signallers or a compensating increase in Signalling personnel are the conditions of successful maintenance of Signalling Communications.

www.ingramcontent.com/pod-product-compliance
Lightning Source LLC
Chambersburg PA
CBHW051719040426
42446CB00008B/964